The Depth of Waves

A collection of thoughts and musings

To Mercedes, who's been there for me
in ways no one else has.

Disproportionate Perceptions

I've entered a state of limbo between reality and dreams. I cannot remember what's happened and what's been conjured. People look at me with worry, when I tell them I thought our conversation wasn't real.

I can no longer tell the difference. I am a collection of everything that was and ever could be.

Fall to Their Knees

I'm tired of trying. Trying to be the better person. Being the one who apologizes, and forgives, and *relents.* Why must it always be me?

I don't wish to try anymore. I want to be the one forgiven, the one fought for, the one who is chased after. Let me be harsh and cruel. Let someone love me for it.

Let them fall to their knees, and beg me to give them just one touch. I've often wondered if the likes of me make it possible to be sought after.

There's a deep hidden desire of
romanticism that pleas it to be so.
But I doubt, and haven't seen it.

The Sea Knows Me

I wish to marry the sea. For the water world would not hurt me the way a man knows how to.

I would not care if its depths drowned me. It would not ache as badly as what could've been. I would sail every ocean, farther and farther away from those who have burned a hole where my heart once was.

The sea would not care how broken I am. As long as I can steer, she'll accept me. When I say I wish to marry the sea, I mean I

wish to live as free as the waves
on her surface.

Exploring the Oregon coast.

Shaking Depths

The horrifying jump in your chest when you start to be perceived. The lodge in your throat when you realize you're starting to *feel.*

Oh to love and never lose. To jump and never miss. But that's a mere dream. Reality is restlessness.

A shaking in your hands that does not belong. It is the uncomfortable realm of hoping that is fruitless.

Escapism

I thought of who I am and who I must be. The horrible truth of knowing I am fascinated by the deep and dark secrets of other worlds.

That I am entranced by the impossible. A fixation on what cannot be. Every day, I lock a little more of myself away in a safe.

How much more of me is left? Soon enough I will be merely a casing of a person, a shell of an individual. As I look in the mirror, I can already see it. Lifeless eyes

that I have, and a hollow voice.
How much longer before there is
nothing left?

Human Nature

I didn't want to want. A part of me wishes I had a heart of steel, one that didn't notice if someone left or not. What was the point of all this want?

For another chance, for another opportunity of higher feeling? Life should not hinge on someone else caring for you. You should be enough for you. No one else.

So why do we hope? Why do we crave touch and affection and to *matter?* It is our nature.

We were designed to want. To yearn for more than we were given. What a terrible existence. What a horrible fate.

Connections

I was thinking about how important connections are. How every single one of them changes us.

It messes with our trajectory. Losing one can be someone's breaking point. Some pray to forget. Others to remember. To resuscitate.

You can connect with someone on such a deep level that you feel like they are a part of you, and then a year later you wish they'd burn. Then there are some, where

they could do anything and you'd
welcome them back with open
arms.

As long as they love you, you'll
always hold a place for them. Isn't
that terrifying? Doesn't it make
your heart stop for a moment?

Writing to Ease

I feel the vicious need to write every night. To pour out my thoughts in some way to make them seem something other than intangible.

To sort them out, figure out what's real. And what I need to remind myself of. To do that seems unfathomable at times. It's simple things at best.

Like reminders of why I work. Or why I need to live in the moment. And those things matter more to those who become weighed down by daily life.

I'm one who spends the whole day and night worrying about what needs to be done the next day. And then I've wasted a perfectly good day.

I've wasted countless opportunities from the what-ifs or the doubts. And it kills me inside. It eats me up and makes me forget how to act sometimes.

It sucks the life out of my soul, and all that's left is some carcass of a person who's trying to feel whole again.

Is There Time to Change?

So many crushing thoughts spinning in my head. Everything I've ever known has changed and I can rely on it no longer.

I'm left questioning everything, wondering where I belong. There are so many things I feel I must do, and I forget to ask myself why I'm doing them.

I simply don't have time to improve in what I want, and I'm filled with uncertainty and unfamiliarity. There's overwhelming sadness in me at times, not being able to let go of anything.

I always feel drawn to why I *can't* be happy. And there's one question left lurking in my mind - will I ever find peace within myself?

But then, **I must.**

Remembering Mantra

You must remember who you are. Remember what truly inspires you. Remember that the way you look is not important, but you are still captivating in your own way.

Remember to find the good in everyone and be kind to all you meet. Remember to smile and ask questions. Remember to take pictures even if you are embarrassed. Remember to not be ashamed of what you like.

Because you need to connect to those who like you for you. You need to strive to do your best and look for ways to better yourself.

Do not be jealous of what others have. Strive to do what you love. Work hard and be smart about it.

All Will Be Well

All your life, you've been told that we all want the same thing. To settle down, get married, and bear children. This is your future, they tell you. Your greatest joy.

But there are some of us who want more. Sure, you'd like to have a partner in life. Someday. But you are one of the few who realize there's so much in this life that you are capable of on your own.

There's so much to learn, to experience, to be a part of. You are told you're being difficult. That you may remain alone forever if you don't lower your standards. But I am here to tell you otherwise.

Be proud of wanting different. Of being in the minority. I promise you, you'll find someone. You'll find someone who won't lock you up and put you in a cage to look pretty.

There will be another soul out there that wants freedom and adventure and wind in their hair just as much as you. You'll find each other. I'm sure of it. It's okay to wait for that. It's okay to not go with the first, second or third person who is entranced by you.

Wait for the one that sets *your* soul on fire. Set each other's souls on fire. Find that person that you can't wait to see again. That you want to work hard for and run away with. I have faith that you'll find them.

There's Still Time

Maybe you didn't have a great year. Maybe you promised yourself this year would be YOUR year. The year you finally get your life together.

And, twelve months later, it's not been as amazing as you thought it would be. There were some highs, but the lows hit hard. They left you knocked down for a while. But you're alive. You're still kicking and fighting.

That will always mean something. You are still striving for

something better. I don't care
what happened to you that year, I
want you to keep going.

I want you to acknowledge
everything that happened - and
then get on with it. Don't let
yourself fester in all of the things
you didn't accomplish. You will
get there. Not now, maybe not
next year. But you will get there.

So let yourself rest. Allow yourself
to feel everything. And then
continue living, continue striving
for that better life.

A Love Letter to Girls With Broken Hearts

I know. I know you're feeling some indescribable feeling because you're alone now and you have to sit in it. You've been questioning everything. If it was your fault.

If you were too harsh. If you weren't enough for them to stay. But let me tell you, love. You were *more* than enough. You hold the universe in your hands, and for a brief interval, you offered it to someone else.

You took all of that magic and
wanted to share it with another
soul. And, selfishly, they took it.
They snatched it from you,
realizing afterward that they
weren't ready for that kind of
potential.

They will stay with their hands
burning, traveling back and
wasting time. They will try to
ignore how it readily came back
to you, that they weren't eligible
for your power.

And one of these days, they'll see
you rise to those stars. Maybe they
won't care, maybe they'll drag at

your feet begging for another touch of your wondrous world.

But for the love of God, don't give them that chance. No. Show them what they've given up. How capable you are, my dear. How awe-inspiring you will become. With a mind so unique and its own that others quiver at their reflection.

You will become so many things to so many people. A friend. A mentor. A lover. Family. A role model. This will be but a grain of sand in your life. Don't let this grief fester and irritate you.

Remember how utterly beautiful you are. An anomaly of a woman, God saw you. He saw what you're capable of. How could he let you become tied down? No, he freed you.

He gave you the opportunity to reach out and grasp something bigger than life. My love, don't look back. Not at what you lost. You didn't lose. You were spared.

Kindred Spirits

It's okay if you don't have your own people yet. Sometimes it takes a lifetime to find your kindred spirits. Or your bosom friends.

Don't settle, and don't try to be something that you are not. Stay true to who you are. If we are not our whole selves, what else is there? That may at times be your only comfort.

But there will always be people cheering you on. People you

sometimes forget about, but you must keep them in mind.

Live in the moment, and remember to always find the good. Wherever you may be.

My best friend and I dancing on the terrace of a castle.

So Long Ago

I seem to dream of a different time. Where there are fields stretched out and windmills in the distance out the window beside my bed.

There's a road out the other window that leads to a small town with friendly people. There's cinnamon and nutmeg in the air, and the leaves are bursting with yellows, oranges, and reds.

There's laughter downstairs, where my mother is making an apple pie and brewing coffee. My father is outside lighting up a fire while we expect friends to come over.

My sister is giggling in the front yard chasing our black cat with eyes that look like pumpkins.

I'm in the middle of it all - with a mug in my hand and contentment in my heart. Friends arrive and we sit around the fire roasting marshmallows and telling stories.

Our faces are lit by the flames, and we can see the stars come out. We can see our orange cat in the bay window, and the cows are huddled together behind us as

the cold night creeps up on them.
We all say our goodbyes and go
back inside, and we shower the
smoke out of our hair.

We all huddle up on the couches
and watch a movie while eating
pie, and we're all so tired we
climb upstairs.

There's a smile on our faces as we
drift off into sleep. One day those
memories will be so distant that
they'll seem like dreams.

They're so fresh still and make my
heart ache for a simpler time.
When nothing hurt.

No Resolution

Not all things are meant to have a breakthrough or a resolution. Some thoughts and perceptions stay and burn through your mind and never change. And maybe it's not supposed to be okay, but you also become so set in an idea that it's as real as a fact.

You know it's as strong as the sun coming up every morning. And some things hurt and scar you, but as hard as you try to change, it's always there. It never leaves.

And so sometimes we as humans
have to accept that in certain
areas of life, we might never have
a breakthrough - or get better.

38

You Made It at 21

I made it. We both did, you and I. This is another year you got through alive.

So many things happened this year. Going to faraway places. Finally visiting those friends who are a creative hurricane, the ones who have been with you throughout the pandemic. But there was loss, too.

People who have been in this thing called your life for years. Ones you'll miss despite yourself. You saw your first love get married. And it broke your heart. You still miss him sometimes, the little imp.

You became your own person again, away from the grief. It still sticks its ugly head in, but you finally have good days again. You're slowly recovering; it's been a tough journey.

You can drink now, but probably won't very often. There's a lot going on in that mind of yours, but you're alive, and that's the important thing.

You're still kicking and fighting,
and that will always mean
something.

Hope Persists

Life is becoming hopeful again. There's fog in the distance and a crisp quality to the air. The leaves have taken on that lovely mix of amber and gold.

When it rains, the world is left with the scent of petrichor and shine. I can read and never think of reality. A perpetual state of dreaming.

When my hair collects dew outside of the inn I keep, I realize *I don't care.*

The music grows softer, and my
mind can finally rest.

Piratical

Pirates and their treasure clad me in their wear. I want to look like all the places I've been to. Rings on my fingers, shining with memories. The clothes that hang from me are a piece of lost history, both mine and the others before me who made them and wore them.

I want to escape to the sea, breathe in the balmy salty air, and realize I'm home. I want to feel the breeze graze my skin, filling me with life. I want to read books

when the sun starts to dance
around my room.

I want to sit with my dog and tell
him he's loved. I want my friends
to feel so special they beam. I
want to move with graceful
intention. I want to feel free and
live every day with the joy of a
child.

Let the ache from years ago and
days from last week roll off my
back, back into the dust we came
from. I want my hair to be wild
with braids and charms and my
neck to be adorned with
mementos.

I want to run and laugh and
dance and scream all at the same
time. I want to *be*.

Honey & Tea

It was late and the stars were out, and I could just make out your outline as you searched our shelves for a copy of *Peter Pan.*

I asked you to read to me. It was a frequent thing when I would have a rough day. You'd prop yourself up on the pillows waiting for me to melt into you, and then you'd open up the book. As soon as you'd speak I'd feel at peace. Your voice as soothing as honey.

I'd listen to you read until I fell asleep, admiring the way the candlelight hit your soft curls. Then you'd put the book aside, wrap your arms around me, and say silent prayers for the both of us.

You'd trace your name in my curves and maybe brush your fingers through my short wispy hair. I'd rise to the smell of tea, which I often related to your smell as well.

You'd be at the table with a cuppa waiting for me, and I'd be delighted to see your fluttering smile where your eyes close slightly. You wrap your arms

around my waist and kiss my
temple. I sigh in contentment.

Only to wake.

Numb Blockings

I've lost the motivation to write. I'm in a moment of time that seems to have slowed down. I take a step back, wondering how it all could've gone so wrong.

How I've ended up in the position I'm in. Where it feels like a prison I'm desperately trying to get out of. Like I'm pleading guilty to whatever made the universe put me here.

I no longer cry. I'm past the point of feeling. It's all numb. I realize there's no coming back and

there's nothing I can do. That
feeling haunts me at night. There
are little slivers of hope here and
there, but soon enough they fade
away.

What am I to do? How am I to
carry on? Nothing will suffice. I'm
left to my own company and
reasonings. To the higher powers
in life where I confide, and only
in them do I find comfort.

The Stars Remind Me of You

I'll never forget when I took my sister to her first observatory. During the time we were watching *Roswell*, it was one of those things we had bonded over. I had planned the night meticulously.

We started off by ordering cheap fast food and driving over an hour to the college-owned observatory, where we played *Under the Milky Way Tonight*. That song will always take me back to that moment of us singing along in the car,

makeup and hair done just to
look at the stars.

The night hadn't even been clear
enough to see anything in the sky,
and my sister was probably more
bored than she would've admitted
at the time, but we both had huge
grins on our faces as the teacher
opened the dome and spun it
around.

We were enamored with the
telescope and memorabilia
everywhere. The building had
stars engraved into the ceiling,
with curtains made of rich deep
blue velvet and embroidered
planets. We wandered around
their library together, looking at

meteorites and astronomic photography.

It felt like we had transported ourselves to the past, ten or twenty years. We both wore crystals around our necks, with manes of curls, and a touch of gypsy grace. Our souvenirs for the night were little *NASA* posters with various depictions.

Maybe it wasn't the coolest thing I could've shown her, and she probably would've rather hung out with her best friend that night, but it was some sort of curiosity we shared. I can't quite remember doing anything together after that.

It was a one-night wonder sort of
thing, and maybe that's why I
can't help but hold onto it. To me,
it was special - sentimental even.
And I think even now every time I
hear that song, or see stars in the
sky, I think of her.

The observatory's library.

When Someone Leaves

What happens when you lose friends and lovers? What's left? What happens when you have so much love to give, but it's left floating in open space? You reach a state of living that seems unfulfilling.

You go on experiencing and experiencing, but there's no one to turn your head to and say, *'Did you see that too? Does it make you feel what I feel?'*

You've heard how it's a dangerous thing to be alone, but we know there's little choice for some of us.

So what do you do? What do you
do when you've faced betrayal
time and time again? You write.
You become so comfortable with
yourself that you learn to enjoy
being alone. You find out new
things about the inner workings
of your mind, and it's like taking a
clock apart.

Seeing how it all works together,
and we tinker with it. We find new
hobbies to enjoy. Whatever it is,
day by day, you forget. You don't
recall the days you were so lonely
and bitter you let out a sob.

You don't remember missing your almost lovers. Those friends that said they'd stick around forever. And one day, one day when you are happy with yourself, they'll come.

People will be drawn to you. To your art. To your smile and mystery. Maybe you'll give them a chance. But you are different now. You won't break the next time someone leaves.

Because as heart-wrenching as it is, it's a part of life. And the amazing thing about life is, it goes

on. That feeling of hopelessness
will run from you soon enough.

Heart Clenching

What is it about stories that take hold of me, leaving me gasping for air? The tales of love and despair and hope send me to tears.

Seeing the gravity of a situation, the sheer *feeling* exuding from these works of fiction never escapes me. I think of them all, I think of them in moments of drifting.

Why does something not of our world make us brim with overwhelming empathy and yearning and desperation? Is it as simple as relying so heavily on escapism?

I was told once that it's because every one of them are our everlasting companions. When everyone else leaves, stories *remain.*

They will always be there, even when it hurts. What we feel for them is what we crave.

Will You Ever Come Back?

Five years ago I would've never thought that there'd be a day when we wouldn't speak. More has changed than stayed the same. Our past selves might as well be separate people entirely.

Now when you enter a room, my heart stops. I don't know where to turn, and I have the insatiable feeling that you'd rather I pretend you're not there. How can I?

How can I when we used to sleep in the same bed and reveal our

deepest secrets to one another
under the disguise of darkness?
How can I when we'd sing
together on the car rides home,
laughing and staring out the
windows?

How can I when we used to say
we'd move out together and travel
the world? How can I when I
know you better than all your new
friends and lover? How can I
when we were together more
often than not?

How can I when you came to me
after I almost took my own life,
tears streaming down your face,

clinging to me? Begging me to stay?

And there's a dull ache in me knowing I secretly wish you'd talk to me again. Not the pleasantries we so often do. Sometimes I almost think you'll wrap your arms around me once more and tell me we're fine.

That all the hurt and pain I've given to you and you've given to me is worth it, because *we're okay.*

And maybe I wasted a few tears thinking we could be close again. Thinking that you'd realize you needed me. I don't think I could ever stop hoping. Because despite knowing better, I still love you.

I worry I always will. You'll always be the first person who *saw me*. So don't hate me for wondering if you'll ever come back.

Tug & Pull

I'm a walking contradiction. A constellation of everything I've ever yearned to be. The lines blur and I wonder where I'm headed all too often. And truthfully I don't think I could be loved in this world.

I'm all too much in my own head. At once kindness to swift seething rage. Craving for what was never here nor there.

What can I possibly accomplish that will satisfy this insatiable hunger?

Abhorrently Known

I know what it is to be wretched.
To be told you're on the verge of
something else. To be warned to
reign yourself in. I've begun to
wonder if I am deplorable.

Contemptible for how I think.
How I operate. My own
stubbornness scares me
sometimes. I've always held onto
things with both fists, gripping
with white knuckles.

For as long as I can remember
I've been entirely too much for
others. But then I've known souls

who share in my whimsies, and to
be understood is a barely
concealed yearning.

Pain Produces Kindness

Perhaps kindness comes from
pain. Pain from being shunned,
and used, and manipulated.

There is an agony that clenches at
your heart, with the knowledge
that others could feel what you
have endured. And even what you
have not.

To think of all the conflicts of
what can be tolerated is infinite.
All this to say, for what you have
suffered, you have done well. If
no one has told you before, I am
telling you now.

Unfortunate Stranger

Who can explain this loneliness where no one *understands?* They are not perceiving me right. They take me for a fool. A wild creature who does not know the right path.

I talk to them, and it's not what it was. I hug my dog, and a sadness fills my bones knowing I'll love him forever but he will soon forget me. His eyes full of love and joy. How long will I have that?

And the lifeguards, I can't tell how much is pain and how much

is love. A soul slipping away from
a life, into a void that fails to fill
what used to be.

The Impending Future

I sometimes wonder if the depths of what I feel will be my downfall. If they are right, and I care for you more than you do for me.

I think about how if I lose you - if you are to be one more person to add to the list of those who have left, I don't know if I have it in me to pick up the pieces.

Perhaps I will rot in a corner and forget what the ache feels like when laughter comes.

Love with Bite Marks

Everything I have ever loved has bite marks. Holding on with vice, afraid they'll escape me. I don't know moderation. If anything, I fear her. Caught between abandonment and catching those fleeting feelings.

Nothing is forever. That is the travesty of it all. Perhaps all I am is a pyre. The harder I try to prolong the inevitable, the deeper the scars. It never leaves. Cursed to feel more than what will ever be felt on my behalf.

A breath of mockery.

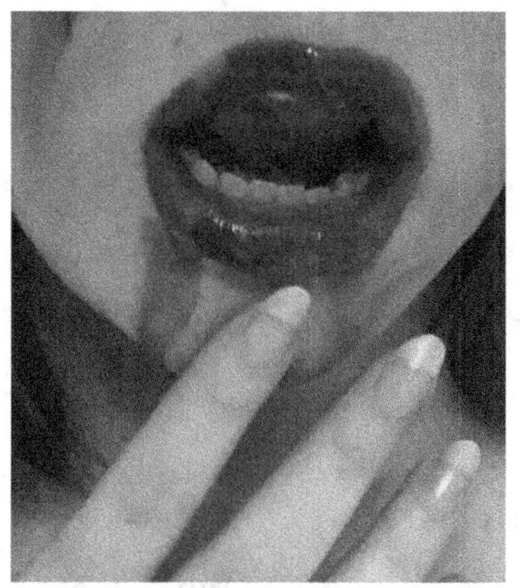

Fragile Optimism

Perhaps it is forward of me to say you are teaching me how to love again. But I have not bared myself to others in such a long time. I may never have done so in this feral way.

The recollection of us pouring over music in your car, dissecting the lyrics and the meanings and the mere ferocity of human emotion. The way you brought your hand out, a silent unbearing.

I grasped yours, and suddenly our fingers intertwined. When was the

last time someone simply held my
hand? With no ulterior motive?
Not to get at me, or beg for more,
or as a guilt trip, but truly as a
sign of connection. You could not
have known.

I could not say the words out
loud. How I recalled the moment
the following nights, wondering if
this too would turn sinister. But I
hope. God do I hope.

I hope you are wildly different.
That perhaps once in this life, this
fragile thing will not turn to
poison.

Separate Matters

A master of deceit. A fragment
between beckonings. Do I fool
you? Or are my own misgivings as
evident as they are in the mirror?

A vicious cycle of concealment
into a bleeding heart.

A Contradictory Constellation

Sometimes I'm an adventurer, a soul with no ties and a world brimming with danger and smoke.

Sometimes I am divine feminine, torn white skirts and tousled hair as I make my way through the fields that have nipped at my ankles.

There are even times I am a gory thing, a beast locked away in the dark draped in crimson and black.

Between each of these are a
million other anomalies.

A vast collection of personas that
have been crudely stitched
together to make a person.

Sunflowers

My sister is summer in a bottle. Açaí bowls full of color and a warm breeze through the trees.

She is music incarnate and the feeling of touching something soft. Her freckles map out a constellation we have yet to discover, but once you've seen them it's impossible to forget their array.

Her smile is the stuff of fairytales, her fingers splattered with paint. It is no wonder her favorite flowers are sunflowers - yet

somehow she outshines even
them.

My ethereal sister in a sunflower field
soon after her graduation.

To Love Is to Fear

I am afraid to fall in love. I am no better than a fool, a lackluster charm in the back of a velvet box.

I think of what it means to be human - we were designed to be accompanied. To isolate is to go against our very instinct. And yet that is how I have so often lived.

The solitude is a balm over my soul, a familiar and safe existence. To love is something that has always scared me. To let you in, to show that I am just another pearl in the sea.

Dream Girl

I am better off alone, the vile creature that I am. Do not come to me expecting compliance and pixie dust.

I am evil. I am every bad thought you've ever had. My claws scratch at my cage, and I can't help the howls that rip me apart.

You want something fleeting, and I want to devour and consume. I am nothing more than a knife, a sharp surface waiting to cut and tear you open. My tears are a product of rust.

The thorn in my side was you.

Am I Not Worth It?

None of it is fair. The peace I chase after. The temporary contentment I fill myself with—a placeholder.

Within me is a rage so profound it seeps from the gaping wounds I have inflicted upon myself.

Why must I yearn for something more? But perhaps I should be asking, why can't I have it?

What makes it out of reach? To feel your touch against my skin, to

feel as though I am the very
reason someone else breathes.

I want it all. That has always been
my problem.

Let me dance with the other parts
of my soul under the stars, the fire
illuminating our faces.

Let me belong to someone else,
the way I belong to the sea. Let
them read to me on a quiet
summer afternoon, with the waves
whispering sweet nothings close
by.

Do I not deserve a grand life?
Must I always bite and tug at the
things I want?

No More Card Games

I'm tired of the game. I want to be
kissed. I want to be wrapped up
in you, safe from the world.

I want to lay my legs over yours
and read into the hazy hours of
the afternoon.

I want to feel your fingertips graze
my arms absently.

I want to hear your deep laughs
fill the air, squeezing at my heart
like they so often did.

I want your cologne to waft
around me, warm and comforting.

I want, I want, I want.

The Color Red

Women and blood have always been so closely connected. It flows through all of us, the life source that twines us together.

But we have always been more intimate with it, haven't we? Has there not been a sort of comfort in seeing red rivulets flow freely?

Surely the act of waiting to close a wound just to see how much you can hurt is not a unique experience.

Have we not always grasped at
things so tightly they bleed? Is
that not our instinct? We paint
our nails the shade of
pomegranates and line our lips
with the tint of cherries.

We have always loved the
decadence of being needed, being
vital to live.

Even Nature Lacks Solitude

These days I spend my time
outside, trying to fill the void you
left behind. I read of a woman
traveling the West Coast, but
there are undercurrents of
melancholy with everything she
does. Her husband is long gone.

Does life not lose some of its zest
when one is alone?

I hear the birds sing and the trees
rustle and cannot help the envy

that even nature has found its
companions.

To Try Again

Few have understood my soul.
What makes up my longings and
sufferings. I've been told I'll find
it again if I simply *"get out there."*

You quoted Dostoevsky to me,
and I realized I had not felt seen
before that moment. I told you of
my dreams and you played along.

We talked of seeing
Shakespeare's plays and putting
our books together. We could read
stories to our children that filled
us with wonder.

You wanted to hold me in a way I
had only yearned for. To try again
feels strange and tiresome.

You Shouldn't Say Those Things

My friends are sick of hearing your name. But you talked to me about what our three kids would look like, and I find myself thinking of little else.

Would they have your freckles? Would they have blue eyes, brown hair, or brown eyes and blonde hair?

Would they have your sharp teeth? My lips or nose? Would we read them *Peter Rabbit* or *Winnie the Pooh* first? Would you teach them how to play the piano?

You talked of splaying your hand on my stomach and kissing me there. If I talk of you, it's only because you are what I think of when I wake… and the one I want when I fall asleep.

The poets have said it all before. I used to find them foolish.

Someone New

I tried talking to someone new
today. I saw their hands, but yours
are what I think of still.

I try to picture myself with this
new person, but my heart churns
uncomfortably. It wants you. Only
you. What have you done to me?

You've severed something in me,
and now it belongs to you. I am
missing something now, as you
carry it around mindlessly.

My pillows remain tear-stained,
catching up my aching dreams.

I Cannot Forget You

I don't want to remember you longer than I knew you. You've infected me like a virus — an incurable disease.

The scenarios come unconsciously. Of what it would be to be loved by you. Cherished, even.

The agony of always wanting you. I find you in every song, every book, every movie. I find you in fleeting moments, and I'll have to pretend it doesn't send a pang through me.

Searching

Reading between the lines has
become my pastime. Searching
for messages in bottles.

You have thrown me away, but the
music you play is full of heartache
and sorrow.

I want to ask what you thought of
the book you were reading, last
we spoke. Instead, I sit in my
room alone, wondering what I
have done.

A Passing Whimsy

Do you think of me at all? Have you ever tossed and turned in the late hours of the night, because of me?

Do you still have pictures of me? Are there sketches of me in your notepad, drawn in charcoal and messy from your hands brushing against the paper?

Do you find me in what you read, what you hear while driving down the highway?

Or was I a passing whimsy—just another means to an end? It is devastating to think that you became a possible future to me, but I was practically nothing more than a distraction to you.

Even worse to know that should you come back six months, a year, even two or three.... I would still let you.

Two Paths

I am at a crossroads. There are two paths forward. One consists of familiarity, and the other is unknown - terrifying and new.

To leave everything I've ever known, to start a new life is the most daunting thing I've considered doing. And yet, to stay in the confined cell I've made myself seems worse.

Comfortable as it is, it is not possible to grow as things have been. Something must give. I am terrified. I will miss this tiny

speck of the world I have known.
But if I am to succeed, if I am to
have a fighting chance, then the
unknown is the path I *must* take.

"Just Leave Me Be"

I write to you from unknown numbers just to tell you I miss you. You say you miss me too, even though you don't know who's on the other end.

I keep a notebook of all the things I wish I could tell you, and even the thought of that makes me want to curl in on myself.

You are unaware. It's no wonder that these days the memory of you is hazy; a vision underwater.

Yet I still write to you. As if you'll answer. As if you know.

Please Love Me As I Am

I am tired of conditional love.
Love that lasts a month or two, or
love that relies on complacency.

Why can I not be loved as I am?
Is that so horrible a task? Will I
ever be loved under all these
layers?

Is it possible to peel back my
exterior, for someone to stay even
for the twisted and battered parts
of my soul? The less than savory?

My yearning has rotted away at
the good and desirable.

I Hate To See Your Heart Break

Your best friend died a few days ago. When I found out I felt something in me constrict. My heart goes out to you, even though we haven't talked in months.

I hate to think you are more alone in this world. I wish I could help soothe the pain. I wish you'd come to me and tell me yourself. Instead, I learned from your cousin.

Instead, I watch from a distance, across the world, hoping you and your family are alright.

You may not love me, but I am too familiar with the makings of your soul to pretend I don't care that you are hurting.

My fingers itch, wanting to write to you. Even though you would not reply. Wanting to tell you I'm sorry. Wanting to comfort you. He looked like you, you know.

He was another one of your cousins, that much I know. I wonder if his son will also look like you.

Will it be like looking in a mirror? Will you look out for his wife and child? I hope you do. I hope you remember how fleeting life is, but that there's hope.

Mostly, I hope you're okay.

Only A Placeholder

Every time I close my eyes I hear your voice again. Telling me you couldn't trust me.

The truth is I was never more than a plaything to you. Wanting to talk into the small hours of the night just because we liked the same things.

You saw a pretty thing to toy with, and I saw someone I could love. That was my fault.

Although I know this numbness
will fade eventually, it's hard not
to feel used. To feel damaged.

The light in my eyes hasn't come
back yet. It will someday. It's only
natural for me to wonder, why am
I always the practice and never
the endgame?

I have acted like a dog, begging to
be loved too many times.

Acknowledgments

Putting thoughts out in the world that were once held tightly in my hands is a scary concept. A feat that could not have happened without my people. There's a few I'd like to thank.

To my parents, for their endless words of encouragement. To Micah Peters, who has been a second pair of eyes on my writings and offered help where she can. To Jackie Dowell, my hype woman and fellow lover of content with a dark twist.

To Jasmine Stanway, someone who's been with me through it all.

To Mercedes Bauman, who never made me feel stupid for all of my big feelings and needing validation. You've always understood me.

I could truly thank countless others. Every time I finish a project, it is with the help of so many lovely people.